Enchanted Forest

AND OTHER POEMS

Rachel Ermutlu

Contents

For my wonderful husband, Dan. Thank you for loving
me through all my struggles.

Imaginative Poetry

<u>Enchanted Forest</u>

I.

Exploring the forest

There is a luscious scent of lavender

The fragrance overwhelms me as I

Breathe in

Trees are comprised of leaves of violet, gold, and cerulean

A blue bird chirps,

"hello" at me

As I extend my arm he comes to

Rest upon it

And we explore the

Colorful forest together

II.

On our walk more animals join us

There is a fawn with dots of white along her back

She asks the bluebird where we are going

He says, "wherever the forest leads us"

A mother rabbit with her babies hops along beside us

Then I see a pink horse with a white horn on her head

"Are you a unicorn?" I ask excitedly

"Of course, what else would I be?"

"I have never seen a unicorn"

"Follow me and you'll see even more

Magical creatures"

III.

As I follow the magical unicorn

I am in awe

As we pass the colorful trees

I see tiny fairies of the most

Vibrant colors

Flying around

A fairy encompassed of pink, yellow and green

Tells us to follow her to the

Enchanted castle

IV.

I'm overwhelmed with excitement
As we keep strolling through the forest
We meet violet bumblebees
Who share their lavender honey with us
There is a lion with a majestic roar
Who steps aside when we get to the
Enchanted castle

V.

The castle is gargantuan
I have never seen a building like it
It is at least one hundred stories tall
And I can't tell where it begins or
Where it ends
It has an abundance of windows
Many are stained glass
It is a lovely lavender color
With a door teal in color
And white trim
I say, "can we go in?"

VI.

Inside the castle
The beauty is

ENCHANTED FOREST

Ethereal
My smile reaches my eyes
It has never been this big
There is a winding staircase
That is a pristine white
At the top of the stairs
I stand in the gallery and look down at all the
Magical creatures

<u>The Butterfly</u>

She sat in the green grass picking yellow dandelions
A beautiful butterfly landed on the flowery weed in her
hand
Then it flew away
She yelled, "butterfly!"
As she waited for it to come back
The butterfly comprised of orange, pink, yellow, and green
flew back and said to my daughter, "follow me"
As she followed the butterfly she marveled at the colors
Not only on its wings but on everything around her
She passed the yellow slide connected to the yellow swing
As she followed it deep into the woods, they passed trees
every shade of green
She walked on dirt many different shades of black and
brown with her pretty pink shoes
She loved watching the birds that were blue, brown, and
red
She wondered where the butterfly was leading her
Suddenly the butterfly stopped at an enchanted tree
This tree was blue instead of green
The butterfly flew up into the lovely leaves of azure
It said again, "follow me"

Suddenly a winding staircase came down from the tree
She excitedly climbed up the stairs
As she followed the butterfly into the tree, she saw an
abundance of flowers and all the fruit snacks she could
dream of

RACHEL ERMUTLU

Enchanted Rose

Title inspired by Beauty and the Beast

What will happen if I touch it?

Will all my dreams be fulfilled?

Or will venom spit from it

So I am slowly killed

Maybe it will give me whatever I will

Could it give me my deepest longing?

Something that is sure to thrill

Or will it start dawning

On me

That this is killing me

Clearly not thrilling me

Will it give me my heart's desire?

Or will it forever be haunting

Me?

Will it send me into flames of fire?

I wonder how it will go?

Should I touch this beautiful rose?

The Staircase

As she meanders up the

Winding staircase of ivory

She rubs her hand on the ornate railing

She knows this antique of a house

Has been abandoned

For quite some time

She wonders who walked

On these stairs

Long ago

Was it home to a prince or lord

Or just someone wealthy?

Did they have children

Who tried to slide down the railing

Or were they childless?

Did they love each other

Or did they just pretend?

So many questions arise as she strides down the

Beautiful

Dusty

Staircase

<u>The Golden Typewriter</u>

There is a typewriter

Spray-painted gold

Is it to hide rust?

It definitely needs

A good dusting

It is beautiful

It was filled with numerous words

Poured out from

Different hearts

Of imaginative writers

Impostor Syndrome and Mental Health

<u>Fine</u>

He asks how she is

"Always fine" is what she says

She can't reveal

The pain she feels

Inside

So she continually says

"I'm fine"

<u>Not a Race</u>

Life is not a race

Stop trying to chase

Someone else's dreams

Just so you can fit in

She has her dream job

He published five books

She got married and had her first baby

You think, *could it please be my turn, maybe?*

We all live life at different paces

You don't need to feel caught in stasis

Please, remember, life is not a race

<u>Real</u>

Please don't say

Mental illness is fake

We have come such a long way

So many people didn't get help

They didn't realize they were unwell

A chemical imbalance is not a sin

Please, don't say that it is

We were doing so well at ending the stigma

Please don't make this another enigma

Mental illness is real

Please, accept this so it doesn't steal

More and more and more lives

Mental health is so important

Please don't miss the warnings

Mental illness is real

Please

Let everyone

Have a chance

To heal

<u>If Only</u>

If only

I had her ruby red lips

And his beautiful eyes of azure

If only I had

This person's

Successful career

If only I had

More and more and more

Maybe then I'd be happy.

Will material things

And better looks

Ever satisfy?

Not according to anyone

From any age of time

ENCHANTED FOREST

<u>Am I a Poet?</u>
Is it poems that I write?
Or just random nonsense that's in
My mind
Maybe I write just for me
But I'd be lying if I said
It doesn't matter what
Others think
Of my poetry
Is it even poetry?
Or just words I write to keep my sanity?
Is it fraudulent
To call myself a poet?
Or do I just not know how to
Own it.

<u>Compliments and Criticism</u>
Why do I have so much anxiety
Going to write at a cafe
I used to do this so frequently
Is my monthly flow of blood
Exacerbating my anxiety
Or is it being fueled by too much caffeine?
I have low self-esteem
I wonder if anyone will like my writing
But even when people love it
I wonder if they're being honest
How can I handle criticism
If I can't even handle
compliments?

<u>Labyrinth</u>

There's a maze inside my mind

It says you don't know how to write

Then

Wait

Yes, you do

You have such raw honesty

And a gift of creativity

Then

No

Your writing sucks

Throw it in the trash

No-one wants to read it

How do I free

My mind from this

Prison

Of a

Labyrinth?

<u>Loneliness</u>

Philippians 4:11 ESV "Not that I am speaking of being in need, for I have learned in whatever situation I am to be content."

Is it a feeling?

Or has it become a way of life

To not interact in person

And only do it online

You scroll on your phone

Looking for a mate

You think, *I just need someone to love me*

And I will never again be lonely

<u>Imposter Syndrome</u>

Am I a writer?

Or do I just write?

Am I too honest

About my brokenness?

Am I too critical

Of myself?

<u>Symmetry</u>
What is beautiful?
When we are completely
Symmetrical?
If so, who at all has beauty?
Anyone?
How boring would life be
If we were all just
Symmetry?

<u>Insecurity</u>

My insecurity has come to rest
In this knot inside my chest
It tells me you're not good enough
You don't know how to write stuff
No-one cares what you have to say
My confidence fades to gray
Insecurity overwhelms my brain
And says, *what do you know?*
Again and again

<u>Inadequate</u>
Am I the person
To write this book?
Am I the right mom
For my kids?
Am I the right wife
For my husband?
Am I the friend my friends need?
Would they be better off without me?
Should I volunteer at a homeless shelter?
Maybe, someone else could do it better
Should I drive my son home from school?
In the pick-up line I feel a fool
Can I do any of this?
I often feel
Inadequate

<u>Pretender</u>

I know how to write

Is what I'm thinking

People like to read

What I have to say

But they actually don't care

Do they?

Will anyone read this?

Does it matter?

If my writing isn't lauded

They won't realize I'm a fraud

Maybe I'm an author

Or maybe I am just

Pretending

To be one

<u>Panic Attack?</u>

The pain in my stomach is overwhelming me

Is it the potato I just ate?

Or my anxiety?

I feel extremely hot and sweaty

What the heck is wrong with me?

Why can't I handle

Criticism?

Why am I so sensitive?

Why do I care

So much

What others

Think of me?

It's okay that probably not

Everyone will like

My poetry

<u>My Belly</u>

My daughter asks, "where is your belly?"

I lift up my shirt and just see fat

So long ago, it used to be flat

Will it ever again go back to that?

I trace the stretch marks on my skin

And wonder how I got these things

Is it from the babies I carried?

I had two difficult pregnancies

Should my fat and stretch marks be hated?

Or should they, maybe, be celebrated?

<u>Silhouette</u>

She sees the shape of her body
As she looks in the mirror
Her stomach feels all knotty
She wonders how she got here?
She sees her silhouette
And is disappointed with the shape
She thinks, *how much fatter could I get?*
She tries to combat the hate
She feels for herself
But she doesn't know how
She doesn't realize she is unwell
Her brain is saying, *ow*
Her heart says she's unlovable
She doesn't realize she is beautiful

<u>Comparison</u>

Why don't I look like her?

Why can't I cook like him?

Her hair is always perfect

And she is paper thin

His food is so exquisite

Mine is just mediocre

Her make-up is done just right

My make-up days are over

She wears a veil of confidence

I feel like I am less and less

He is so intelligent

I wonder if he is a savant

I'm so absent-minded I forget my own name

Why can't I keep it together like him?

Why do we compare?

We all have parts we don't like to share

I don't need to be someone else

I just need to be myself

<u>Naïve</u>

She was lonely and naïve
When she was 23
Looking for love in all the wrong places
Dealing with problems not everyone faces
Looking to others to improve her self-esteem
Trying not to burst at the seams
But she learned recently
When she turned 30
Her self-esteem is not from others
Not even her husband or her mother
God loves her and that's what matters
Even when her whole world shatters
She's seeing herself the way God does
So she always remembers she is loved

<u>Façade</u>

She paints a smile on her face

She wears a lovely dress of lace

She talks and laughs with everyone

Her make-up is flawlessly done

Her legs are a perfect shade of bronze

Her hair is a stylish shade of blonde

She is the most beautiful woman I have ever seen

How wonderfully happy she must be...?

<u>Drowning</u>

You're going down, down deep

Into the anemone

The salty water fills your lungs

You splash and splash to get back up

You feel seaweed on your feet

You start to admit defeat

You slowly start giving in

To the ocean

Wait...

There is a rope being lowered

You grab on with hope

You are lifted

To the surface

<u>Running</u>

You can keep running

Wondering what is coming

You can stop moving

Wondering if you're losing

Your mind

Your thoughts are scrambled like grapes on a vine

What is real?

What is not?

Has the collision of reality and fantasy just begun?

What are you running from?

<u>Future Self</u>

My books will be sold all over the world

My poems will help people know

They are not alone

I will be loved and adored

No-one will ever get bored

Of what I have to say

I will help whoever comes my way

Everyone will have my books on their shelves

These are my hopes for my future self

A Picture of Love

Love

Love is...

Hot coffee in the morning

Love is...

A trip to the bookstore

Love is...

Having a hand to hold

Love is...

Growing old

Together

<u>For the Record</u>

I love you for the record

Serenade me and I'll press record

As you sing to me my heart is melting, I think 5,826 times

is the record

I dream of you tenderly rubbing my back as we listen to

our favorite record

Your lips on mine fill me with passion, in my mind, I record

I treasure you for the record

I write poetry about my affections, in my journal, I record

I'm more infatuated with you than reading and writing,

the depth of my love could never be recorded

You always make me laugh, is there a new record?

You are my favorite person; I adore you for the record

In Love

I am so blessed with you
You're the only man for me
I am so in love with you
Our love is so true
I'm glad you and me became we
I am so blessed with you
You make my cheeks flush with rouge
Seeing you fills me with glee
I am so in love with you
I always wondered who
Would be the man for me
I am so blessed with you
I like kissing you times two
My affection is as vast as the sea
I am so in love with you
Thanks for saying, "I do"
You still make my heart skip a beat
I am so blessed with you
I am so in love with you

<u>The One</u>

She feels so weak
She can hardly speak
He walks by again
Her heart stops beating
She wishes she knew how to flirt
Because he looks so good in that flannel shirt
She imagines stroking his beard
And hopes she's not too weird
For him to talk to her
He says something and her mind is a blur
She can hardly breathe
She thinks, *is he talking to me?*
She manages to mumble something
And hopes this is the one thing
He won't remember
So they can be together
If she can get the words off her tongue
She hopes he will be the one

<u>Real Love</u>

Our love sometimes feels like magic
Even if we've gone through times that were tragic
You make me feel so seen
And support whatever I dream
You encourage me in all things
And are so good-looking
You're my best friend and lover
There will never be another
Man I love like you
I'm so glad you're my *I do*
Even if we've had to heal
Our love is
Perfectly
Magically
Breathtakingly
Real

<u>Stay</u>

She wonders if he will stay

He seems so genuine

But so many men have walked away

Maybe she should stop dating them like a religion

She wonders if she has an addiction

To love... or is it lust?

She should probably change her vision

Of who she can trust

And hopefully not be discarded like dust

She wonders what love really means

And thinks that he must

Like more than her good genes

And possibly love her

Does he? Or is there another?

He Loves You

Is this love?
You silently wonder
As your heart beats as loud as thunder
You find it hard to catch your breath
You think he could be the one unless
He finds someone better than you
Which would be quite simple to do
Someone with more self-confidence
Who hasn't built an invisible fence
Around the depths of her soul
Someone who knows their goals
Who's bold enough to step into the unknown
And not be terrified of being alone
He says, "I love you"
You think, *is this true?*
It is.
He is so in love with you

<u>Love Hurts</u>

Does love cause pain?
I love you so much
I hurt when you hurt
Your pain causes me pain
Sometimes love hurts

The Pain of Heartbreak

<u>Broken Promises</u>

Why make a promise you never intended to keep?

Why would you cause so many souls to weep?

Was it for money, love, or power?

Or because you enjoy leaving a sour

Taste in my mouth

Maybe you had the best intentions

Was it a promise you tried to keep?

But it just made you weep and weep

Because you craved so much power

And didn't care about the sour

Taste in my mouth

Please, tell me you have good intentions

Are these all lies, or can I keep

Hoping I will no longer weep

Your lust for power

Has made our lives extremely sour

You love the taste of world domination on your mouth

You have disastrous intentions

Maybe I can lock you up in a keep

But I can't handle hearing you weep

I wish I had more power

But our love has gone sour

Will it ever improve, or will you forever have the kiss of

deceit on your mouth?

I loved you with the best intentions

Why'd you tear out my heart with the shattered promises

you said you'd keep?

It seems all I do is weep, and weep, and weep

All you cared about was power

It didn't matter that your love affair made me sour

I don't believe a word that comes out of your mouth

I still don't know your intentions

ENCHANTED FOREST

Never promises to keep

Maybe, you enjoy making me weep?

More and more and more power

Until the whole world has gone sour

You love controlling things with just one word from your

mouth

I think these are not good intentions

I think all that we'll keep is broken promises that make me

weep

Your only love is for power, I can't stand how sour

Your mouth is. I hate your intentions

<u>Just Another Tuesday</u>

It was just another Tuesday

When she got into his truck

He said, "should we have some fun?"

And she said, "yes"

It was just another Tuesday

When she realized she was late

She waited another week

Then she took a test

Two pink lines let her know she would be blessed

This isn't the way she wanted to be blessed with her first

baby

She called the guy she hadn't talked to lately

It was just another Tuesday

When he said, "it's a lie"

When she sent him proof

He said, "I believe you're pregnant, I just don't believe it's

mine"

She said, "you're the only one"

He said, "no way, you're too much fun"

She calls and texts and calls until he blocks her number

How could someone be so cruel? Is all she has to wonder

She doesn't tell anyone until it's obvious

She never imagined having her first child like this
It was just another Tuesday
When her mom asks if she's pregnant
She says, "yes, and I don't know where the father went"
It was just another Tuesday
When she went to the hospital
Her mom held her hand as she had her baby girl
She wishes her daughter could meet her dad
But she knows
Their Heavenly Father
Has a plan

RACHEL ERMUTLU

<u>The Window</u>

By the window she sits

Waiting...

Waiting...

Waiting...

For someone

Will he ever come?

Days turn into weeks

Months turn into years

She slowly has to realize her fears

He is gone

By the window she sits

Waiting...

Waiting...

<u>Heartbreaker</u>

She sent him a handwritten letter

It was full of seductive charm

He read it in the rainy weather

As a drop of water trickled down his arm

He smiled at the love in the air

Her letter was so flirtatious

But then she disappeared to who knows where

And he felt caught in stasis

He pondered why she led him on

She learned she was afraid of love

He thought she only wanted fun

She never felt good enough

He kept trying to forget her

She knew she was a heartbreaker

<u>Playing with Fire</u>

We are taught not to play with fire

So why is it often our heart's desire?

Our attempts at love can be in vain

When all they bring is pain upon pain

You slowly lose pieces of yourself

When being used by someone else

Your feelings aren't reciprocated

How did you end up so jaded?

Your problems may seem very dire

But you can overcome the fire

<u>The Call</u>

She called him on the phone
She said she'd rather be alone
He said, "why?
I thought I was the guy
For you"
He thought they had something
Special
He even bought a ring
She said they weren't that serious
Which only makes him curious
What the *I love yous* were all about
He slowly begins to doubt
Himself
He thinks he will never love anyone else
He wonders why it hurts so much
He remembers every single touch
He doesn't want to be alone
Why'd she call him on the phone?

RACHEL ERMUTLU

<u>A Haze</u>

As she strolls by the river

She is reminded of him

And she wonders when

She started to shiver

Her memories are like arrows in a quiver

She was so in love with him

Her heart is breaking from within

She is slowly withering

She tries to hold back her tears

But they gradually stream

Down her face

She wonders how many years

She was caught in between

And stuck in a haze

<u>Unbroken</u>

Is he in love with someone else?

Is she like a dusty book that's been left on a shelf?

She believed they would be forever entwined

But for some reason, he changed his mind

She thinks, *am I too ordinary?*

She thought he was the man she would marry

But he has already moved on

To a very beautiful blonde

She thinks, *I could never be as hot as her*

Her heart is breaking, and it hurts

She decides to never love again

So her heart will remain unbroken

<u>Forgotten Existence</u>

Why did this love fade?

She wonders *why this masquerade?*

She waits by the phone for his call

And wonders if she was ever loved at all

She feels extremely dumb

For thinking he was the one

She smells his cologne on her sweater

And wonders why they're not together

She thinks, *why is love like this?*

Slowly she realizes

He forgot

She exists

Faith Transforms

<u>Forgiveness Cinquain</u>

Listen

You're forgiven

Accept the love of God

His love is unfathomable

Breathe in

<u>Faith and Trust</u>

Psalms 27:1 ESV

"The Lord is my light and my salvation; whom shall I fear?
The Lord is the stronghold of my life; of whom shall I be
afraid?"

In what or whom

Do I put my trust?

Am I putting it in my husband

My friends

Or my stuff?

Faith and trust in earthly things

Will never satisfy

Our needs can always be

Found in

Christ

<u>Free</u>
I've been set
Free
From my sin
And shame
My sin can no longer
Define me
My Savior has set me
Free
I have been
Forgiven

<u>Never Satisfied</u>

Ecclesiastes 5:10 ESV *"He who loves money will not be sat-*
isfied with money, nor he who loves wealth with his income:
this also is vanity."
Are you content?
Are you satisfied?
Is the secret to happiness classified?
Maybe if you make one more dollar
Your satisfaction will never falter
But you keep making more and more
And still wanting more and more
The answer must be in a new romance
Or having your career exponentially advance
You think, *why am I never content?*
I have everything I could ever want
Will I ever be satisfied?
What is the real meaning of life?

<u>Insignificant</u>
Do you ever feel
Insignificant?
Wondering if God
Could ever use you
Thinking you're too broken
Wondering
Does God really use broken things?
Thinking you're not qualified
No matter how small you feel
There's a God who is bigger
He can use you
If you
Just
Trust
In Him

<u>Forgiven</u>

I messed up

Again

And again

And again

I'm so unworthy

I've sinned horrendously

Again

And again

And again

God could never love a freak like me

Could He?

Could I be forgiven?

Could I ever go to heaven?

God pours out his grace and love

On you, and me, and anyone

Who turns to Him

With love and repentance

<u>Beautiful Stories</u>
Is your story full of
Love and life
Or is it full of
Grief and strife
Or maybe
Probably
A little bit of both?
Do you have trauma and tragedy in your past?
Would past mistakes make me gasp?
Do you wonder if there's truly a
Love that lasts?
I have found an
Everlasting love
In Jesus
My Savior

<u>The Cross</u>

Inspired by the gospel of John chapters 18 and 19
You were beaten and mocked
You did it just for me
You love us all so much; how could we not see?
Your best friend betrayed you with a symbol of love
You knew it was coming, but it must have hurt so much
They called you a liar and even a blasphemer
But we know that you are our Redeemer
You were whipped
And whipped
And whipped
Although, you were innocent
They mocked you with a crown of thorns and a purple
robe
You gave yourself for everyone, all around the globe
They shouted, "crucify him!"
Would I have shouted with them?
They pounded nails through your wrists

ENCHANTED FOREST

I can't fathom the pain
You died for the sins of everyone
Your death was not in vain
Thank you, Jesus for dying on that tree
Thank you, Jesus for giving your life for me

<u>Innocence</u>
You feel naïve
You feel left out
You slowly begin to doubt
Your decision
Pain is not what you envisioned
With your vow to stay pure
This scrutiny is painful to endure
At eighteen
You feel
You're the only one
Who hasn't
Given your whole self to
Someone
But don't worry
Your life is only just beginning
Don't be ashamed of
Your innocence

Mom life

Love So Deep

Why do our kids have to go through struggles?

Are they still able to be fixed with snuggles?

My son's pain fills my heart with sorrow

Please, can I borrow

Your hurting

So you don't have to

Endure it

I know you are still learning

But I keep yearning

To make your pain my own

So you don't need to face it alone

<u>Real Men Cry</u>
Big boys don't cry, they say
How archaic is that?
Boy, cry if you need to
Boy, cry if you are sad
Learn healthy ways to express anger
So you don't become violent
Don't hold in your feelings until you burst
Boy, cry if you need to

<u>To My Son</u>
I love your creativity
And your expansive imagination
I love your gift of empathy
Even if it contributes to your
Complex feelings
I love when you snuggle me watching a show
Even if it's an episode I very much loathe
I love your curiosity about God and heavenly things
It's wonderful watching your faith begin
I love how much you care for your sister
I pray you always have a good relationship with her
I love you more than words can express
I'm so thankful I have been
Blessed

<u>How do Moms Find Time to Write?</u>
My daughter who is
Age 2
Is clingier than a
Baby kangaroo
She wishes there was a pouch to climb
Into
I say, "Do you want to watch a show?"
She says, "Yes, mom come
Snuggle"
I start to walk away, and she says
"Hey!"
"Hey!"
"Hey!"
"Mommy, you need to stay"
She feels so sad if I'm not in the same room as her
How are moms
Successful
Writers?

<u>In the Moment</u>

You're never too old

To play a board game

To sit around a table

And laugh with your friends

To disconnect from screens

And be present

In the moment

The Beauty of Seasons

<u>Windy Day</u>
It stirs the leaves
It is the breeze
I feel slip
Through my hair
It's the fresh air
I inhale
As it brushes against
My rosy cheeks

<u>Summer Loves</u>

As I wash the dirt

Off my feet

I'm reminded of my former summer loves

My summer loves weren't boys

Who I was crushing on

Although, there were a few of those

My summer loves were

Camping

Bonfires at night

Swimming at twilight

Playing on the trampoline

And

Running around in my

Bare feet

<u>Rainy Day</u>

On this gloomy

Windy day

Filled with lots of rain

It is lovely

To snuggle up with a book

And a frothy latte

Flavored with chocolate

And the sweetness of strawberries

As I sit

By the window

<u>Christmas Morning</u>

My son comes in our room and

Awakens me

He jumps up and down on the bed

And shouts

"Mom!"

"Dad!"

"It's Christmas! It's Christmas! It's Christmas!"

We slowly sit up and rub the sleep from our eyes

I say, "Kiddo, please be quiet"

I walk upstairs to get his sister

He runs behind and shouts

"It's Christmas! It's Christmas! It's Christmas!"

My heart is full of joy as I watch them open their first gifts

His sister is struggling so he helps her when he's done with

his

After her first gift my 2-year-old is bored

She looks out the window and sees flecks of white falling

from the sky

Her face has that special glow

As she shouts

"Snow!"

"Snow!"

"Snow!"
I look outside and think, *oh no, it's cold*
But the trees full of snow look so beautiful
My husband and I snuggle as we watch our kids
We all have child-like joy on
Christmas morning

<u>Inner Child</u>

Gallivanting in the rain

Is so

Exhilarating

I am bubbly with excitement

As I skip around catching

Fireflies

There's a smile on my face as the jar glows with their

Luminous light

While I swim in the water at twilight

The scent of chlorine reminds me of my

Teenage years

I pick a bouquet of dandelions

And hand them to my son

He gives one to his sister

As we sit in the grass I smile

As I observe how my kids

Help me find my

Inner child

RACHEL ERMUTLU

<u>Wildflowers</u>

I pick the lilies from the field
And weave them through my hair
I place a crown of vibrant colors
On top of my head

<u>Summer Magic</u>
Fresh watermelon in the
Summertime
Is so magical it's
Sublime
I love savoring a sweet
Red pepper
As I enjoy the
Sunny weather
The smell of sunscreen is sticky and sweet
As I feel the grass tickle my
Bare feet
I love hearing the serene chirps
As my daughter yells, "It's a bird!"
I could never list every reason
Why Summer is my
Favorite season

Acknowledgements

First, I'd like to thank God. I'd like to thank Him for saving me from myself when I was suicidal and for every opportunity he has given me since then. I'd like to thank my husband, Dan, for supporting me in everything I do and helping me with technology that makes me want to cry (exaggerating... a little). I'd like to thank Elle McCarrick for editing my book and being so encouraging. If anyone else needs an editor, you can look Elle up on Linkedin. I'd like to thank Cait Palmiter for doing my book cover: it is perfect! If anyone else needs a graphic designer, you can find Cait on her website: www.caitpalmiter.com. I'd like to thank my parents, Amy Huss and David Huss, for loving me and encouraging me. I'd also like to thank my mom for reading everything I write and proofreading anything I ask her to. I'd like to thank Kim Johnson for talking with me about writing and giving me ideas and suggestions. I'd like to thank my friend and sister-in-law, Kate Ermutlu, for encouraging me to publish this book and for telling me my poems were good when I felt like they were crap. I'd like to thank my kids for the ideas they gave me as they were playing. I'd also like to thank anyone who may have influenced my writing in any way. And thank you, reader, for buying and reading my book. If you liked it, please leave a review on Amazon or Goodreads.

About the author

Rachel Ermutlu enjoys expressing feelings and creativity through her poetry. She has found writing to be helpful for her mental health. When she's not writing, she loves hanging out with her family, playing board games, drinking lattes, and reading as many books as possible. She lives in the Lansing area with her husband, and their two children.